MARTYN TURNER was born in Wanstead, Essex, in 1948, only a short bus ride from Leyton Orient's ground at Brisbane Road. He reluctantly gave up the chance to attend all their home matches in perpetuity when he took the slightly more attractive option of moving to Belfast in 1967 at the start of the Troubles to attend university. From 1971 to 1976 he was co-editor of the Northern Ireland independent review, *Fortnight*. Since 1976 he has been the contributing political cartoonist of the *Irish Times* in Dublin.

His previous books are: *The Book* (1983), *Illuminations* (1986), *A Fistful of Dáilers* (1987), *Not Viking Likely* (1988), *Heavy Weather* (1989), *The Guy Who Won the Tour de France* (1991), *The Long Goodbye* (1992), *Politics et al* (1992), *The Odd Couple* (1994), *Pack Up Your Troubles* (1995) and *The Noble Art of Politics* (1996).

He was named Commentator of the Year by the Irish Media Awards in 1995 and received an honorary doctorate from the University of Ulster in 1998. Both of these awards are guarded, day and night, by a pack of highly trained Irish red setters deep in the countryside of the Republic of Ireland (where, coincidentally, he lives).

# MARTYN TURNER

# BRACE YOURSELF, BRIDGE IT!

## A GUIDE TO IRISH POLITICAL RELATIONSHIPS
## 1996–1998

In association with
Irish Times Books

THE
BLACKSTAFF
PRESS

BELFAST

*for the one and only Jean*

Almost all of the cartoons herein first appeared in the world's
greatest newspaper, the *Irish Times*. A few were commissioned by
the *Express on Sunday,* which just goes to prove that I'll do any-
thing to get paid in sterling. My cartoons are sometimes syndicated
round the world by The Cartoonists' and Writers' Syndicate,
New York . . . bless 'em.

First published in 1998 by
The Blackstaff Press Limited
3 Galway Park, Dundonald, Belfast BT16 2AN, Northern Ireland
in association with
Irish Times Books

© Text and cartoons, Martyn Turner, 1998
© Foreword, Jeff Danziger, 1998
All rights reserved

Martyn Turner has asserted his right under
the Copyright, Designs and Patents Act 1988 to be identified
as the author of this work.

Printed by The Guernsey Press Company Limited

A CIP catalogue record for this book
is available from the British Library

ISBN 0-85640-639-2

# FOREWORD

A friend in New England who followed agriculture rather than the arts once explained to me that sculpture was fairly easy. If, for example, you were doing a statue like Michelangelo's *David*, all you had to do was to get a big block of stone and then chip away everything that didn't look like Dave. There was no arguing the point, especially since he was right, but I allowed that you had to know in advance which were the right chips of stone and which weren't. It was a matter of vision. Not unlike cartooning.

You start with a piece of intimidatingly blank paper. You want to produce something evocative, instructive, infuriating or funny. It's there somewhere. Pencils are helpful because they are so soft and forgiving. They smudge easily and are erasable. You dither around trying to find the thing you think you see in the blinding whiteness of the paper. But the pencil sketch does not tell everything. Its co-operative nature is unreliable and fuzzy. You may think the drawing has said something when it has only hinted at it. The ink is the test, applied with a steel nib, sharp and uncompromising like a scalpel. Or with a brush, capable of either a supremely clever line or an embarrassing blob. There are clever blobs but they are rare.

I like the comparison to sculpture, since the absolutism of black ink and white paper is like that between stone and air. The task in cartooning is to fool the eye, to make it see mottled flesh and slicked down hair and other real things like surging water and searing fire. All with the most reductive graphic elements. Masterful sculpture stands up to centuries of weather and abuse, rape and pillage. Masterful cartoon art-work stands up to the brutalities of newspaper printing, endless xeroxing and the blocky reformulations of the Internet. How do you arrange the squiggles and lines so people think they've seen a real thing, and then make them laugh at it or shudder in anticipation? It's a heartbreak when it fails, but a delight when it works.

All of this is in Martyn Turner's work. But the delight in Martyn's ideas is his willingness to arrange his artwork around a subtle point. This takes some bravery and most people in this field don't try it, since the low belly laugh is more reliable. Trying to talk an editor into playing to nuance rather than bombast is a hard sell. What I most like is the way all Martyn's politicians, Irish and otherwise, look out of the page with the same expression they must have when they wake up in the morning and first behold their faces in the mirror. This is mild hell for all mankind, but worse for politicians and partisans trying to square the evasions of yesterday and the tergiversations yet to come. Martyn is best at catching the uncomfortable moment when the guy is caught, when today's pronouncement begins 'um . . . er . . . you see . . .'. Which is what I mean about the vision behind the little ink lines. You can read in those faces the unsureness, the anticipation for whether or not the lie will fly. Of course it's just a few lines scratched on paper, but it must be more. After all, it does make some of them very angry. And the rest of us pleased.

JEFF DANZIGER
NEW YORK
AUGUST 1998

Jeff Danziger's political cartoons are distributed by the *Los Angeles Times* syndicate.

INTRODUCTION

I was going to call this book 'The Bridges of Thirty-Two Counties', starring Meryl Streep as Mary McAleese and Clint Eastwood as, well, I couldn't think of anyone for Clint to play, so that was the end of that. Then there was 'Bridge Work', which involved drawing a lot of people with gleaming teeth and there aren't too many gleaming smiles in the Irish political establishment. No go there, then. So it became 'Brace Yourself, Bridge It'. Heaven knows what that means. If you're not sure, ask your mother.

For thirty years I've been hanging round this gaff, drawing these pictures, waiting for a chance to do something different. I'd like to do a political cartoon on Northern Ireland. Not a sectarian cartoon, not a tribal cartoon, not a violence cartoon, not a historical cartoon, nor a 'cultural' cartoon. I'd like to do a political cartoon. Something about politics: the redistribution of wealth, the health service, dustbin collections, left wing/right wing sort of things. The stuff political life is supposed to be about. But you won't find any like that on Northern Ireland in this collection of cartoons, I'm afraid. But maybe, just maybe, in the next collection, if there is one, a few years down the line when the Assembly is assembled, the First Minister is ministering and the Cross Border bodies are very cross indeed.

With luck and universal good will . . . no, sorry, this is Northern Ireland I'm writing about . . . with luck, Nor'n Ir'n will develop a political life just like we have down here in the Republic where I happily live. (I happily lived in the North too, in case you were wondering.) This involves setting up numerous tribunals to look into beef fiddles, alleged planning irregularities, payments to politicians, offshore accounts, financial scams, tax scams, and any other scams you can think of. And these tribunals have proved to be an efficient way to redistribute wealth – taking it from the benighted taxpayer and putting it straight into the wallets of barristers and solicitors. It may not be moral, it may not be seemly, but few people get killed, hardly anyone gets burnt out of their home. In fact it remains infinitely entertaining, which, as everyone knows, is the main function of politics these days.

Furthermore, down here our political parties are bent on merging – Labour with Democratic Left, the PDs with Fianna Fáil. Strangely the two conservative populist parties, Fine Gael and Fianna Fáil, have no plans to unite despite their adherence to pretty much the same policies whenever they are in government. It is too soon after the Civil War of almost 80 years ago for such things to be considered. The different sides still remember. The warring sides still stay apart. So take heart Northern Ireland – based on the statistic that one year of civil warfare equals 80 years of political antagonism, the reconciliation of the two sides after 25 years of Troubles cannot be expected to happen for at least 80 times 25 years which is, er, 2,000 years. And a lot can happen in 2,000 years. Look at the last 2,000 years, for example.

It's 2,000 years since the birthday of You Know Who – our excuse for having the millennium – and his laudable, but second-hand, ideas of peace, love, charity, forgiveness, turn-the-other-cheekness, internationalism, intertribalism, brotherhood, sisterhood, and reconciliation. Well, they seemed like good ideas at the time.

Instead of all those virtues we got religion. 'Imagine,' as someone once wrote, 'there's no heaven, and no religion too.' Imagine. No religion. What sort of world would we have had in this neck of the woods? No Crusades. Imagine. No Inquisition, no Henry VIII, no Reformation, no Cromwell, no Sixteen Ninety, no Ascendancy, no Penal Laws, no pogroms, no anti-semitism, no Nineteen Sixteen, no Protestant priests rabble-rousing their supporters and then disowning the violence they roused, no Catholic priests blessing the Lads before they went out on missions, no Bloody Monday Tuesday Wednesday Thursday Friday Saturday Sunday, no Drumcree, no bans on divorce and contraception in the Republic of Ireland, no segregated education, no farcical, absurd, artificially created cultural differences between people, no need to build bridges, no need for political cartoonists. No cartoons to put in this book. No book. No present to give someone for Christmas. Well, actually, no Christmas. Happy Christmas.

MARTYN TURNER

# 1996

The story so far. In America Bill engaged in a spot of gratuitous Iraqi bashing just to help get himself re-elected while his chum Tony, over in England, looked like getting himself elected on the back of gratuitous Tory bashing. An unnecessary exercise as the Tories were quite capable of bashing themselves. In the Republic we began to discover how far businessmen have gone in their selfless support for democracy, paying for the supports, foundations and roofing in politicians' houses and the like. We also enjoyed the spectacle of a government minister bilocating between Wexford and Dublin airport. In the North rumours of ceasefires abounded between the explosions and kneecappings and the good burghers of Ireland pondered the threat from the good burgers of

Ireland as BSE continued to rear its ugly head alongside other ugly bits of the food chain. The North also brought us a new tactic in the continual effort of how to lose friends and influence people – a boycott of Protestant businesses. And that was the good news . . .

.... MY FATHER WAS 66....
...... MY MOTHER was SURPRISED!
HO HO HEE HA
HA HA HO
CHORTLE!
YOU KNOW THE SLOGAN....
New LABOUR.. ......... old SCHOOL TIE!
HA HEE HEE
HO HO HO..HA!
I NEVER KNEW THAT John PRESCOTT...
...... KNEW WORDS THAT LONG!
HA HA HEE
GUFFAW!
HO HEE HA
... AND WE ARE GOING TO....
.... WIN THE ELECTION!
HO HO HO
HEE HEE HEE HA

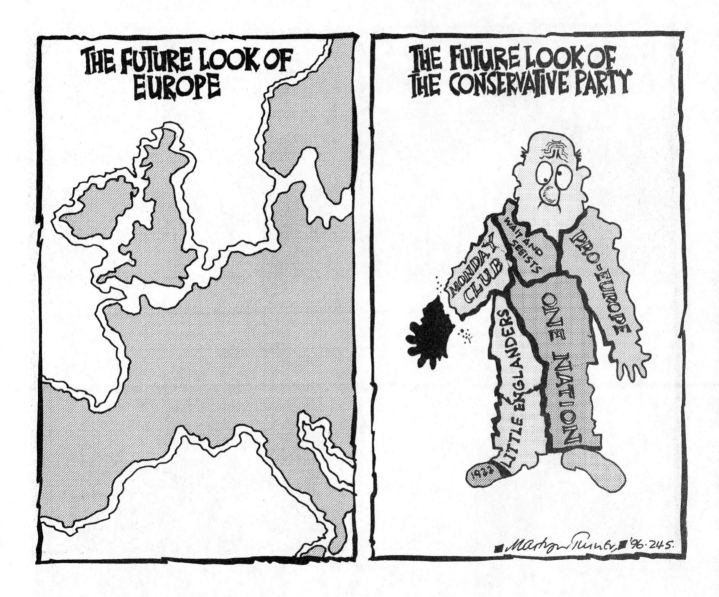

# 1997

It was the year of elections, here, there and everywhere. Mr Haughey elected to not quite come clean over his donations from businessmen. An old friend of Mr Haughey's, Ray Burke, shortly after he had been made Minister for Foreign Affairs, also let us know a little about how business had supported his democratic endeavours via brown envelopes. He resigned from politics. In Britain Tony Blair and New Labour replaced John Major and Old Conservatives. Few people noticed any difference. The IRA declared a cessation of their campaign. A lot of people in Republican areas, broken arms, kneecapped legs and a few murders later, haven't noticed any difference. Not to be outdone, the Orange Order and their supporters treated us all to another Drumcree and demands to walk down the Queen's highway. In England the Old Order demanded to ride down the Queen's

highway, turn left into the countryside and watch dogs rip foxes to pieces. Well, it takes all sorts, unfortunately. Fianna Fáil, elected after promising Zero Tolerance, failed to implement the policy. No one noticed. Mary McAleese survived various smear campaigns to be elected President. She built a bridge to sanity and burnt a small one to the Catholic Church by taking communion with Protestants. The world didn't stop. The Fianna Fáil/PD government introduced a budget aimed to redistribute wealth . . . to the wealthy, who know what to do with it, apparently. William Hague took over the Tory Party. No one noticed. Ruairi Quinn took over from Dick Spring. Brendan Howlin noticed.

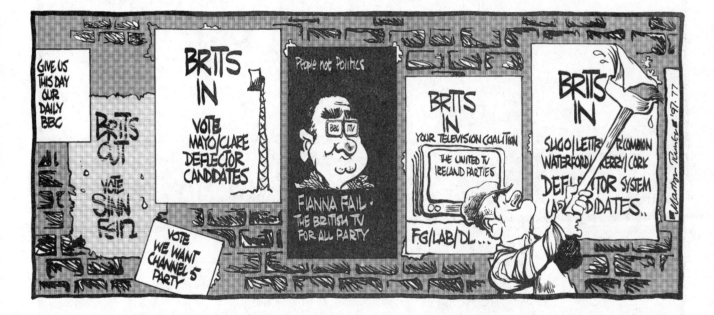

38

N.IRELAND
APRIL 6 RIOT
APRIL 7 BURN
APRIL 8 BOMB
APRIL 9 MARCH
APRIL 10 SHOOT
APRIL 11 BURN
APRIL 12 DEMO
APRIL 13 BOMB
APRIL 14 RIOT
APRIL 15 MARCH
APRIL 16 SHOOT
APRIL 17 BURN
APRIL 18 RIOT
APRIL 20 BURN
APRIL 21 SHOOT
APRIL 22 DEMO
APRIL 23 BURN
APRIL 24 RIOT
APRIL 27 SHOOT
APRIL 28 MARCH
APRIL 29 RIOT
APRIL 30 BURN
MAY 1 VOTE
WAZZAT? V....O....T....E....? VOT... VOTE.. WAZZAT ABOUT THEN?
IT'S DEMOCRACY... NOTHING FOR YOU TO CONCERN YOURSELF WITH...
THE N.I BIGOTS CALENDAR IS SPONSORED BY IGNORANCE, FEAR AND MORE IGNORANCE
'97.76 · THE IRISH TIMES

50

52

At last, a leader with policies and ideas that the **whole** <u>whole</u> Tory Party can agree on......

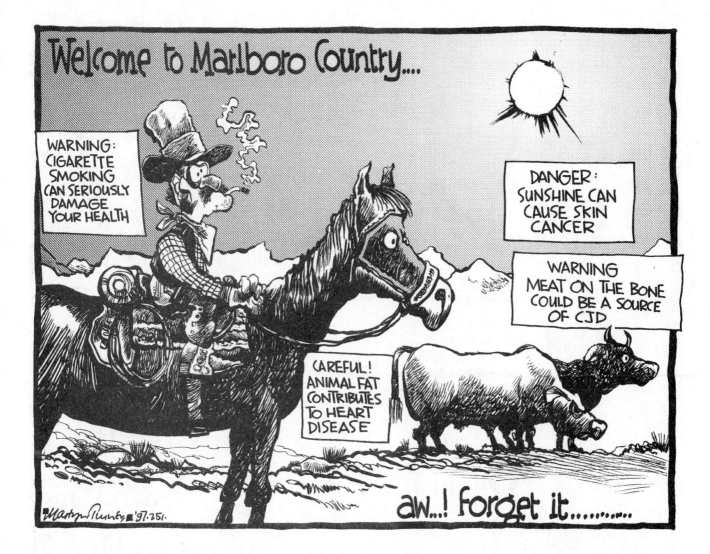

60

PASSING THE BATON.....

74

# 1998

... is the year of the North. There was hardly a day when Northern Ireland wasn't top of the news: cliffhanging talks, cliffhanging cessations, cliffhanging elections and hanging people from cliffs, or the equivalent, when the paramilitaries interpreted 'cessation' to actually mean thugging away as usual. And then there was Drumcree, not quite as usual. For relief we had Mr Clinton, an allegedly serial trouser dropper, which left we cartoonists to ponder whether his private life was any of our business ... for about three seconds. In the Republic we watched the government stay together, after a fashion, and got further revelations into the economics of being a Ray Burke and a Charlie Haughey. India and Pakistan went atomic, Iraq got threatened again, and Israel and Palestine took on the baton of obduracy from Northern Ireland ... which is where we came in ...

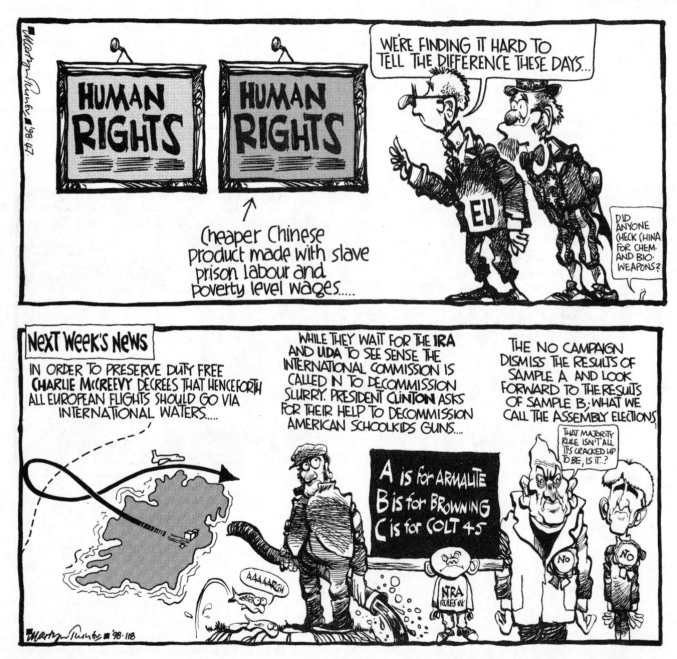

CUT DOTTED LINE FOR SOME HOPE FOR THE FUTURE

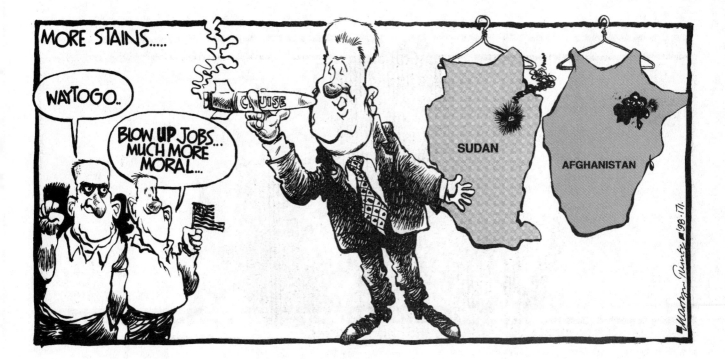